*The way we want
to be at*

TIMPSON
The Quality Service People

THE BOOK OF
TIMPSON VALUES

First published in 2004 by Timpson Limited. © John Timpson 2004.
All rights are reserved. No reproduction, copy or transmission of this publication, whether
in whole or in part, may be made without prior consent of the publisher.

ISBN 0-9547049-2-4

Timpson House Claverton Rd Wythenshawe Manchester M23 9TT
Tel: 0161 946 0200 www.timpson.com
Written by John Timpson CBE. Printed in Great Britain.

The Timpson Attitude

At Timpson people matter, people thrive and people create success.

Our reputation has been earned by people who bring the right attitude and values to work.

This book gives a guide to what makes Timpson people tick!

A small number of our high achievers

LEE NICHOLS

BOB NORTHOVER

SID HUBBARD

KARINA KENNA

GOUY
HAMILTON-FISHER

WINSTON HARRIS

ANDY ROBINSON

PAM MORLAND

Where we are heading

We want to build a team of like minded people who look at life the Timpson way and achieve peak performance.

Team players

PERRY WATKINS

Successful people work for each other. They bring the right attitude to the job and resent anyone who stands in the way of progress.

BILL PLATT

They recognise the work of individuals and are delighted when a team member can celebrate success.

Contract of employment

*We make this commitment to each other and our customers - "**we will deliver world class and amazing service - we will move mountains to make things happen.**"*

Beyond the call of duty

JOHN QUANTRILL

GAIL COBB

JOHN WHELAN

KERRY BURKE

PAUL MYATT

RAB MITCHELL

*Many of our people go well beyond
the extra mile to help their customers
and their colleagues.*

Upside-down Management

We will not stand in the way of anyone who wants to improve our business.

Our staff have the authority to do what they think will best provide an amazing service.

Great inventors

IAN OAKES

DYNAMIC
KEYBOARD
INVENTOR

KELVIN REDDICLIFFE

MEMORIAL
SIGNS
INVENTOR

GLENN EDWARDS

JEWELLERY
REPAIRS
INVENTOR

JOHN HIGGS

SHOE REPAIR
TECHNOLOGY
INVENTOR

TIMPSON VALUES

We are serious about customer care

A TIMPSON VALUE

People come first

We aim to amaze customers with the quality of our service

"Leave them with me, I'll sort out all the problems and give you a ring when they're ready."

We respect others

We believe in candour. Tell everyone everything and tell them the truth

"I'm sorry to tell you, it's not a Rolex!"

If we make a commitment we keep it

"I'll drop them off to you on my way home."

We are accessible and easy to do business with

We work hard

A TIMPSON VALUE

We practice the art of the impossible

A TIMPSON VALUE

We enjoy our work and have fun!

We often celebrate success, but are never satisfied

"I'll get the watch repair cup again next year."

We reward our people properly

THE TIMPSON
PHRASE BOOK

Lead, follow or get out

No internal memos or email – talk to each other eyeball to eyeball

No hierarchy, no pecking order and no politics

No voice mail – just pick up the phone

*Everyone is an individual –
no one is a number*

Come to work with the right attitude.

Customers and suppliers are our most important people

Service is a state of mind

"I'm here to help."   "When is it
                              5 o'clock."

Choose your own job title

*And if possible choose your hours
and pick your place of work.*

Everyone has the right to training

We tell the truth

"The whole truth and nothing but the truth."

Our bosses don't issue orders

"Just let me know when you're ready, I'll leave you to it."

USEFUL PHRASES

We cannot afford the luxury of a bad days business

We like being different from other businesses

We don't blame others –
we just find a solution

"Don't worry, I'll show you how to do it,
then next time you'll know."

We don't want whingers.
Successful people overcome
adversity and make
their own luck

"This idea could be the one that doubles my bonus!"

USEFUL PHRASES

No one likes to work with a moody pessimist

"Cheer up, we've broken last years' record!"

Our highest achievers deserve the biggest pay packet

"All that training has really paid off."

We enjoy being surrounded by buzzy people

We only have two rules

Look the part!

Be 100% honest!

THE BOOK OF
TIMPSON VALUES

World class

*We want a world class performance
– so we need world class people.*

Customers

Customers don't rely on us – we rely on customers. They are doing us a favour by providing our passport to success.

NB. Substitute the word suppliers for customers and read it again.

Truth

*We tell the whole truth to each other,
our customers and suppliers.*

*If someone gets upset with the truth…
…let them. Always say it like it is.*

"You don't sell any extra keys because you look so miserable."

Get better

*We are driven on by the belief that
we can always get better*

Training

Training starts with your apprenticeship and never stops – it will continually reveal more talent than you ever imagined.

Enthusiasm

Enthusiasm is a more valuable asset than money, power or influence.

Enthusiasm is contagious, it brings joy to your colleagues and profit to the business.

"Only £200 for a record week!"

Change

We like change – it's the way to get better and grow our business.

John or James

We can be very efficient but we are always informal.

Everyone is on a first name basis, call "Mr Timpson" John or James.

JAMES & JOHN

Best talent

Our business needs the best talent to be working on its biggest problems and best opportunities – we will continually re-shuffle our team to suit the company.

No voice mail

We answer our own 'phones and are never "in a meeting".

We hate all voice mail it is banned from our business.

Letters

Avoid internal memos — they are cold and often misleading.

The best letters say thank you and are written by hand.

Dear John,
Thank you for the great service, will see you again when I lose my other key!
Regard Mavis

Profit

Everyone is a profit centre in their own right – each individual has the power to make profit for the company.

Expenses

When working, pretend the company's money is your own.

Write your expense claim so it would not embarrass you if it is posted on the notice board.

We don't hire or fire

We don't hire people – we ask people to join our company and help us make it better.

We don't fire people – we ask them to leave and go where they can be more productive.

"You will make an ideal traffic warden."

Success

Success is measured by our cash flow –
more money should come in each
week than goes out.

Promotion

We believe in always promoting from within – but candidates must say "yes" to three vital questions…

…do you want the job?

…can you do the job?

…will you do the job?

Speak your mind

Our people are not afraid to speak their minds – anyone can speak directly to John or James.

"Can I have a word please John?
There is something you ought to know."

Aim high

It is not unreasonable to aim to be world class and legendary.

Problems

We rally round colleagues when they have a problem.

"It's OK Bill, do you need a lift at home!?"

Talk talk

Walking round, making conversation and exchanging gossip are the most important jobs bosses do.

"And the fish was this big...!"

Our values and reputation

*We like to be recognised for our values
and are proud of our reputation.*

THE BOOK OF TIMPSON VALUES

Juggling work and leisure

There is more to life than business.

If you work extra hard, take time off to compensate.

Our motto

If we take care of our people.

They will take care of our business.